I0426048

Department of Homeland Security
Office of Inspector General

Recommended Practices for
Office of Inspectors General
Use of New Media

Council of the
INSPECTORS GENERAL
on INTEGRITY and EFFICIENCY

This report was prepared on behalf of Council of the Inspectors General on Integrity and Efficiency

OIG-11-120   September 2011

September 30, 2011

Preface

At the request of the Council of the Inspectors General on Integrity and Efficiency (CIGIE) Homeland Security Roundtable (HSR) and with the approval of the CIGIE Executive Council, the Department of Homeland Security (DHS) Office of Inspector General (OIG) chaired the New Media Working Group (Working Group), consisting of public affairs specialists, attorneys, information technology (IT) professionals, and other subject matter experts, to assess OIG use of new media.

This report describes current and prospective uses of new media tools in the OIG community and suggests practices that OIGs may use as they consider implementing such tools. It is based on questionnaire responses from Working Group members, survey responses from 39 of the 79 CIGIE members polled, the subject matter expertise of new media specialists, discussions with industry professionals, legal research, and a review of applicable documents.

The recommendations herein have been developed based on the best information available to the Working Group, and have been discussed in draft with the CIGIE HSR. We trust that this report will guide OIGs as they consider the use of new media to further the OIG mission. We express our appreciation to all who contributed to the preparation of this report.

Charles K. Edwards
Acting Inspector General

Table of Contents/Abbreviations

Abbreviations

CIGIE	Council of the Inspectors General on Integrity and Efficiency
CIO	Chief Information Officer
CNCS	Corporation for National and Community Service
DHS	Department of Homeland Security
DOL	Department of Labor
DOT	Department of Transportation

Table of Contents/Abbreviations

ED	Department of Education
FCA	Farm Credit Administration
FISMA	*Federal Information Security Act of 2002*
FY	fiscal year
GAO	Government Accountability Office
GSA	General Services Administration
HSR	Homeland Security Roundtable
HHS	Department of Health and Human Services
IG	Inspector General
IT	information technology
NARA	National Archives and Records Administration
NASA	National Aeronautics and Space Administration
NLRB	National Labor Relations Board
NSF	National Science Foundation
OIG	Office of Inspector General
OMB	Office of Management and Budget
OPM	Office of Personnel Management
RRB	Railroad Retirement Board
SBA	Small Business Administration
TIGTA	Treasury Inspector General for Tax Administration
TOS	terms of service
TVA	Tennessee Valley Authority
USAID	U.S. Agency for International Development
USITC	United States International Trade Commission
USPS	United States Postal Service
VA	Department of Veterans Affairs

Council of the
INSPECTORS GENERAL
on INTEGRITY *and* EFFICIENCY

The CIGIE was statutorily established as an independent entity within the executive branch by the *Inspector General Reform Act of 2008*, Public Law 110-409. The mission of the CIGIE is to

- Address integrity, economy, and effectiveness issues that transcend individual government agencies; and

- Increase the professionalism and effectiveness of personnel by developing policies, standards, and approaches to aid in the establishment of a well-trained and highly skilled workforce in the federal OIG community.

<u>Membership</u>

- All IGs whose offices are established under either section 2 or section 8G of the *Inspector General Act*, or pursuant to other statutory authority (e.g., the Special IGs for Iraq Reconstruction, Afghanistan Reconstruction, and Troubled Asset Relief Program)

- The IG of the Office of the Director of National Intelligence (or at the time of appointment, the IG of the Intelligence Community) and the Central Intelligence Agency

- The IGs of the Government Printing Office, the Library of Congress, the Capitol Police, the Government Accountability Office, and the Architect of the Capitol

- The Controller of the Office of Federal Financial Management

- A senior-level official of the Federal Bureau of Investigation, designated by the Director of the Federal Bureau of Investigation

- The Director of the Office of Government Ethics

- The Special Counsel of the Office of Special Counsel

- The Deputy Director of the Office of Personnel Management

- The Deputy Director for Management of the Office of Management and Budget (OMB)

CIGIE HSR

Since September 11, 2001, protecting our Nation has been a paramount concern of the entire federal establishment. The OIG community plays a significant role in reviewing the performance of agency programs and operations that affect homeland security. To a large extent, this has been accomplished through collaborative efforts among multiple OIGs.

On June 7, 2005, the President's Council on Integrity and Efficiency Vice-Chair established a President's Council on Integrity and Efficiency HSR. The roundtable supports the OIG community by sharing information, identifying best practices, and participating on an ad hoc basis with various external organizations and government entities. The CIGIE New Media Working Group was formed under the auspices of the HSR.

OIG

Department of Homeland Security
Office of Inspector General

Executive Summary

This report presents a snapshot of where Offices of Inspector General stand today regarding the use of new media. It also is an attempt to sensitize the Office of Inspector General community to the ways in which new media tools may help an Office of Inspector General achieve its mission and why an Office of Inspector General needs to be aware of new media developments. Just as the government's adoption of other technologies, such as email and websites, required adaptation, new media's popularity is causing even reluctant government agencies to reconsider their options. Some Offices of Inspector General hesitate, however, because they are concerned about such issues as information security, privacy, and legal oversight. Yet Offices of Inspector General should consider the Open Government Directive issued by the White House on December 8, 2009, which states

> Emerging technologies open new forms of communication between a government and the people. It is important that policies evolve to realize the potential of technology for open government.

With that thought, the Council of the Inspectors General on Integrity and Efficiency New Media Working Group presents and analyzes issues involving emerging technologies that Offices of Inspector General can implement to carry out the President's initiative.

Offices of Inspector General can use external new media tools to disseminate information to host agency staff, Congress, the public, and other stakeholders, as well as to allow various users to interact. Examples of external new media tools include Twitter, Facebook, blogs, and podcasts. In addition, new media can be used internally to communicate and to manage information and knowledge, such as through a collaboration space or wiki. Examples of internal new media tools include SharePoint, SurveyMonkey, and OMB Max. Results from a survey that the Working Group sent to 79 Council of the Inspectors General on Integrity and Efficiency members indicate that about 2 dozen use new media both for internal and external purposes.

Of the 39 Offices of Inspector General responding to the survey, two-thirds reported that they currently use at least one type of new media, while most of the remaining third said they have plans to implement new

OIG

Department of Homeland Security
Office of Inspector General

media or are in the process of doing so. The most common new media tools they are using are SharePoint, Twitter, OMB Max, RSS feeds, and Facebook. Survey responses show that use of new media has effected positive changes. Internally, new media improved communication, information sharing, and collaboration among staff. Externally, new media helped to increase awareness of the office missions, arouse interest in reports and investigations, and drive traffic to websites. Survey results showed that   :

- New media tools are helping Offices of Inspector General both to manage information and knowledge internally and to communicate externally.
- Offices of Inspector General are concerned about information security, privacy issues, and legal oversight.
- New media efforts call for multidisciplinary expertise.
- More education is needed within the Office of Inspector General community.

The report includes six recommendations to Offices of Inspector General and one recommendation to the Council of the Inspectors General on Integrity and Efficiency. The report also includes appendices on legal resources, information security, and tools that certain Offices of Inspector General are using. These appendices are designed to raise awareness of the many issues that Offices of Inspector General should consider and to enable them to reach out to others with more experience.

Background

In fall 2010, the CIGIE HSR asked the IG of DHS to lead a working group to explore new media use among OIGs. CIGIE was aware that many agencies that OIGs oversee either employ new media tools or are planning to do so. CIGIE also recognized that OIG personnel may not be familiar with new media tools or how the government uses them. Therefore, CIGIE sought to create a forum for OIGs to discuss how they can use new media, as well as how they can better oversee their agencies' use of new media. The CIGIE Working Group charter called for members to explore how OIGs could use new media to serve the OIG mission, research legal and information security issues, and discuss recommended practices.

The Working Group began meeting regularly in December 2010. At the outset, subgroups for legal and information security issues began to research their respective issues. Soon thereafter, the Working Group sent a questionnaire to its members to learn about their new media use. After reviewing responses, the Working Group formulated and administered a survey of OIG new media use among 79 CIGIE members. Final responses from 39 OIGs, two-thirds of which identified themselves as new media users, were received in July 2011. The Working Group reviewed the survey results and identified some recommended practices. This report makes six recommendations to OIGs and one recommendation to CIGIE regarding OIG new media use.

What Is New Media?

When people think of "new media," they typically think of such social media platforms as Twitter and Facebook, which reported more than 750 million followers in 2011. But "new media" is in fact much broader and encompasses all forms of electronic, digitalized, and interactive media, including tools that allow interactive communication with an external audience and those used solely internally. New media technically also includes email, but email is not covered in this review because it is already in common use. "External" new media, such as Twitter or Facebook, allows interaction with a public audience, whereas SharePoint and OMB's MAX platform are examples of "internal" new media, which facilitates knowledge management, collaboration, and internal communication.

New media has become firmly established in our society, including the private sector workplace and the government. Through new media, the government can engage the public through diverse means and on a scale never achieved before. New media tools are available to anyone with Internet access, anywhere in the world, at any time of day. New media enables the government to provide improved service to its citizens with prompter responses, greater attention to individual concerns, and overall better customer service. President Obama recognized new media's increasing role within government when he issued his January 2009 *Memorandum on Transparency and Open Government*, which encouraged agencies to "harness new technologies to put information about their operations and decisions online and readily available to the public." In response, many government agencies began to explore and embrace new media tools. But with more involvement comes a need for increased responsibility, accountability, and diligence. Inadvertent misuse of these tools can create significant vulnerabilities and other problems for an OIG.

Some examples of new media tools are the listed below. For a list of some OIGs that use the tools, see appendix B.

Internal Tools

MAX OMB Max: A federal government "private cloud" that allows government employees, government ID-holding contractors, and sponsored contractors to manage and share information and collaborate on interagency projects.

SharePoint: Microsoft software that allows internal Web portals (intranets) for document sharing and search, team collaboration, blogs, and wikis.

Survey tools such as SurveyMonkey: Online survey tools that enable users to create their own Web-based surveys.

WebEx: A Web conferencing tool that combines desktop sharing through a Web browser with phone and video conferencing capabilities, facilitating on-demand collaboration, online meeting, Web conferencing, and video conferencing applications.

Wiki: A type of collaborative workspace on the Web that allows users to contribute or edit content. The best known public example is Wikipedia, but federal agencies can also use the technology.

External Tools

Audio or video podcasts: MP3 audio or video files that may be downloaded from the Internet onto computers or portable listening devices, such as iPods or other MP3 players. Users can listen to or watch podcasts at their convenience.

Blog: A website where bloggers write entries in a diary-like format.

GovDelivery: A "Software as a Service" tool that allows an agency to share information with citizens via emails, text messaging, RSS feeds (see below), and social media.

Facebook: A social networking website that allows users to create a profile and connect with others by "friending" them. The site allows users to post and respond to comments.

IdeaScale: A crowd-sourcing platform that allows users to submit ideas, discuss and refine others' ideas, and rank ideas by preference.

LinkedIn: A business-oriented, professional networking site that allows members to create a professional profile and connect with others.

RSS feed: An abbreviation for Really Simple Syndication, RSS is a way of formatting information so that it is easily read by computers, enabling quick distribution of information to subscribers of a particular website.

Twitter: A microblogging service that allow users to write up to 140-character posts called "tweets," to follow other users who tweet, and to "retweet" those they follow.

YouTube: A video-sharing website on which users can upload, share, and view videos.

Survey Results and Findings

Survey questions sought input on areas such as the reasons why OIGs are using new media, the tools they are using or considering, overall experiences, resources expended, oversight issues, obstacles, metrics, and legal and information security requirements. Results revealed the following:

- New media tools are helping OIGs both to manage information and knowledge internally and to communicate externally.
- OIGs are concerned about information security, privacy issues, and legal oversight.
- New media efforts call for multidisciplinary expertise.
- More education is needed within the OIG community.

The complete survey questions are presented in appendix E.

How OIGs Are Using New Media

Survey results showed that OIGs are using new media for many purposes, including the following:

Required Reporting. OIGs use new media to fulfill and supplement traditional reporting methods for reports and publications, including semiannual reports, top management challenges, and audit and work plans.

Notifying Congress of OIG Work. OIGs are using new media to communicate with Congress. As the Congressional Research Service recently pointed out, many members of Congress now use email, blogs, YouTube channels, Twitter, and Facebook to communicate with their constituents.[1] Members and their staff are attuned to social media and expect to find information about OIGs there, too. New media notifications can link directly to the OIG website, where reports can be viewed and downloaded along with other information and resources.

> *The United States Postal Service (USPS) OIG was one of the first OIGs to embrace social media. Since 2008, it has managed its Pushing the Envelope blog, a Facebook page, and Twitter account. Its Audit Projects page lists all ongoing audits and allows the public to comment online. But the agency is not focusing solely on social media. This OIG's Five-Year Strategic Plan, fiscal year (FY) 2011–FY 2012, makes it clear that in the next five years, it will leverage new media to find even more significant ways to provide value. This includes using new technology to improve its investigations and audits, and continuing to use technology to collect and analyze information. USPS OIG will also develop data-mining models to identify investigative and audit leads. Finally, it will use social media tools to establish "a more interactive professional collaborative environment."*

Resource for Citizens, Policymakers, and Journalists. OIGs use new media to drive traffic to their websites and communicate with citizens, policymakers, and journalists. Although an OIG's website is publicly available, social media capabilities can increase interest and participation. For example, podcasts featured on OIG websites can make the work of OIGs more accessible and user-friendly. Such use of new media tools "support[s] the fundamental democratic role of spreading information about public policy and government operations."[2]

Internal Communication and Collaboration. OIGs use new media tools to collaborate internally, reduce redundancy, facilitate training, and manage information. For example, OIGs use SharePoint, which allows dispersed teams to collaborate on publications and reports. OIGs also use other tools such as WebEx to facilitate meetings, OMB Max to collaborate on a government cloud, and SurveyMonkey to solicit ideas and input from employees.

---

[1] *Social Networking and Constituent Communications: Member Use of Twitter During a Two-Month Period in the 111th Congress*, February 3, 2010.

[2] Id., p. 1.

Investigative Tool. Investigators use social media to locate evidence of crimes, obtain criminal intelligence, gain background information on suspects and victims, generate leads, find assets, and deter crime and wrongdoing.

Data Gathering. Auditors, inspectors, and evaluators use social media to gather information for their work. For example, they pull information from Facebook or LinkedIn to learn about an individual or business. They also can use new media to determine whether the agency under review is leveraging new technologies to disseminate government information, and whether the agency has in place proper controls, appropriate guidance, and effective performance indicators. They can check whether the agency incorporates social media as part of a crisis communications or response plan. Furthermore, they can develop increasingly complex data mining models to identify leads with a high potential for identifying fraud and potential monetary savings. See figure 1 for the reasons OIGs are using new media.

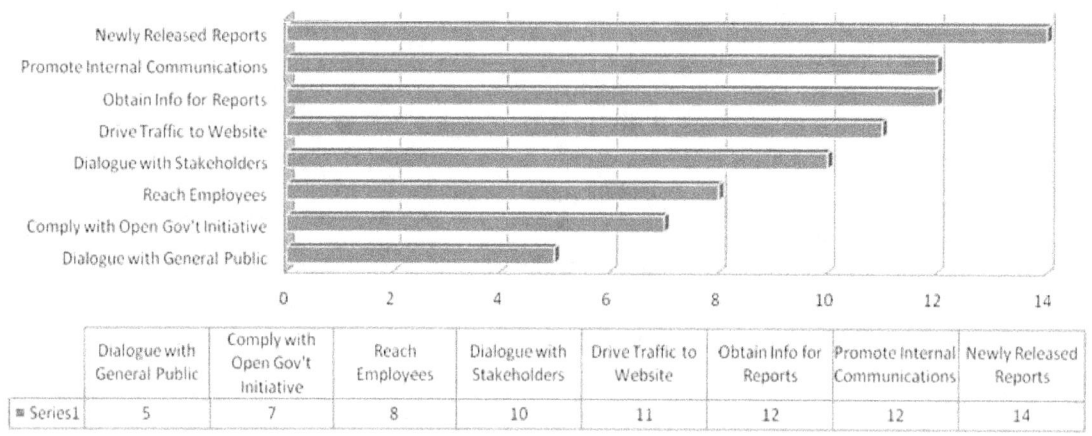

	Dialogue with General Public	Comply with Open Gov't Initiative	Reach Employees	Dialogue with Stakeholders	Drive Traffic to Website	Obtain Info for Reports	Promote Internal Communications	Newly Released Reports
▪ Series1	5	7	8	10	11	12	12	14

Figure 1: Reasons Why OIGs Are Using New Media

NARA OIG Uses Facebook for Investigative Outreach

The National Archives and Records Administration (NARA) OIG uses Facebook to help recover missing documents and other artifacts. Since its creation in May 2010, the NARA OIG's Facebook page has attracted more than 1,500 Facebook friends.
The page is hosted by NARA OIG's Archival Recovery Team, which investigates allegations of stolen or missing federal historical documents. Getting the site operational took several weeks, but maintaining it takes only a few hours each week to post new content and respond to comments.
To date, postings have resulted in six solid investigative leads. Inspector General Paul Brachfield said, "We enlist the American public to be our 'sentinels' in helping us to locate records or artifacts that have been alienated from our holdings and by extension other institutions. Social media serves as a clarion that allows us to spread our message and receive the support of a wide array of people."

New Media Tools Are Helping OIGs Both To Manage Information and Knowledge Internally and To Communicate Externally

New media tools such as SharePoint, OMB Max, and SurveyMonkey are helping OIGs manage information and knowledge internally:

- **OMB Max**. OIGs are using OMB Max to communicate with OMB, comply with *Federal Information Security Act of 2002* (FISMA) reporting, gather and disseminate information internally, and meet the standards of the Open Government Initiative, which involves increasing transparency, participation, and collaboration within the federal government and with the public.

- **SharePoint.** SharePoint is the most popular new media tool among OIGs. It is also the internal media tool that most OIGs are considering. OIGs use it to gather, store, and share information on an intranet; promote internal collaboration; and, in at least one case, encourage staff to use email less.

- **SurveyMonkey.** OIGs are using SurveyMonkey to collect data and to facilitate communication. They use it to administer employee surveys, solicit ideas, and gather feedback on proposed strategies and policies, and also use it externally to gather stakeholder feedback on published evaluation reports. One OIG praised SurveyMonkey for being easy, anonymous, and attractive to survey respondents. The Working Group used SurveyMonkey to conduct its survey.

External new media tools, such as podcasts, RSS feeds, Twitter, and Facebook, are helping OIGs communicate with an external audience. To cite some examples:

- **Podcasts.** OIGs find podcasting to be a simple, inexpensive, quick way to deliver news and information, such as short interviews with senior staff to highlight important work, reports, congressional hearings, and training. One survey respondent commented that the Government Accountability Office (GAO) podcasts inspired that OIG to do something similar.

- **RSS Feeds.** OIGs using RSS feeds to disseminate information have seen increased traffic to their websites and received positive feedback from stakeholders.

- **Twitter and Facebook**. Nine OIGs are using Twitter, and three are using Facebook. These are also the most popular tools that OIGs are

> *A few congressional staff members expressed surprise that we weren't on Twitter, and our involvement on CIGIE's New Media Working Group also led us to revise our position on Twitter.*
>
> *—OIG survey respondent*

considering. Such tools allow the OIG to disseminate information and reports to more targeted audience, including congressional staffers. See figure 2 for the new media tools that OIGs are using and figure 3 for the new media tools that OIGs are considering.

The National Aeronautics and Space Administration (NASA) OIG joined Twitter and Facebook in August 2010 as part of its continuing effort to make OIG products available in a timely manner to a wider audience using a variety of media. NASA OIG uses Twitter and Facebook to update Congress, NASA employees, the media, the public, and the OIG community about the release of OIG reports and other items of interest, such as new projects, letters to Congress, press releases, and semiannual reports. Since launching these services just over a year ago, the OIG has gained approximately 200 Twitter followers and more than 860 Facebook "fans." More than half of the OIG's postings on Facebook have more than 1,000 impressions. Within the same period, the OIG's website has been visited approximately 275,000 times, with visitors downloading information from the site more than 2.8 million times.

NASA OIG also posts on its website brief video overviews of important work products, such as the agency's top management challenges, special investigative reviews, and audit reports. These efforts have increased its visibility and provided new vehicles to disseminate timely information on its activities.

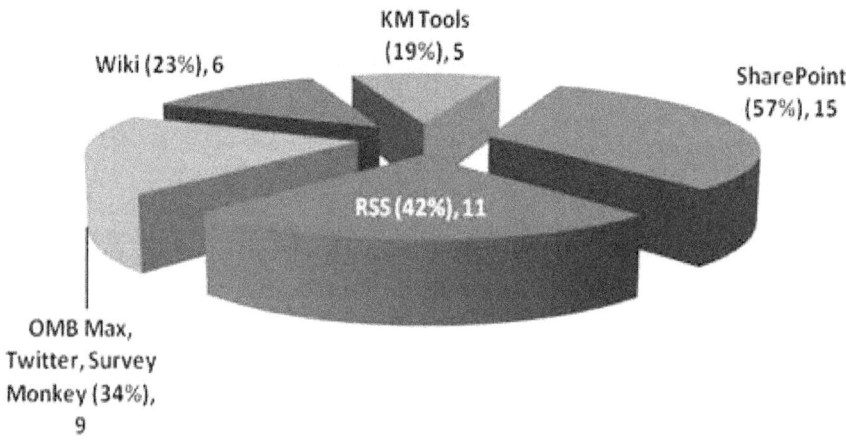

Figure 2: New Media Tools That OIGs Are Using

Tools that OIGs are Considering
(Based on 39 Respondents)

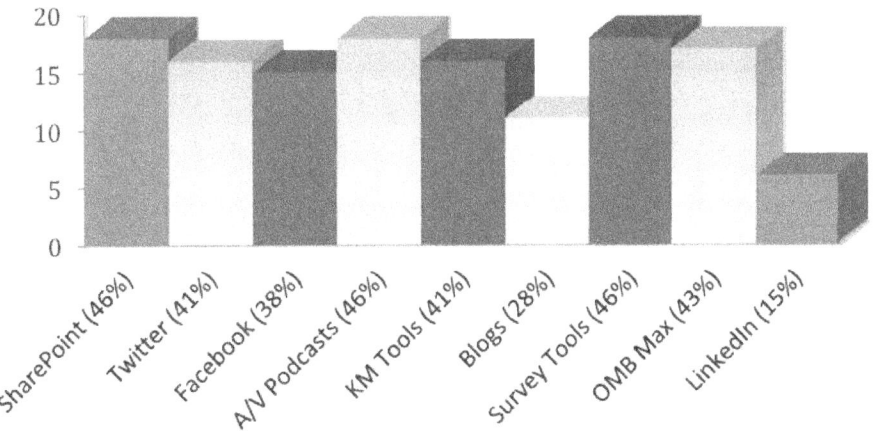

Figure 3: New Media Tools That OIGs Are Considering

OIGs agree that new media can serve the OIG mission in numerous ways. Two-thirds of respondents indicated three or more ways they would like to see their offices use new media (see figure 4). Three-quarters of the respondents would like to see their offices use new media to increase awareness of the OIG. Most also view new media as a way to increase the efficiency and effectiveness of OIG personnel, enhance communication among OIG employees, help recruiting efforts, and facilitate obtaining comments and feedback that may increase the OIG's ability to provide effective oversight. OIGs agree that, when used effectively, new media can help the OIG by

- Providing easy access to reports and projects;
- Educating the public about the OIG and its mission;
- Shaping the perception of the OIG and its work;
- Educating agency employees about fraud, waste, abuse, and mismanagement in the agency;
- Directing agency employees and the public to the OIG Hotline; and
- Increasing transparency within the agency.

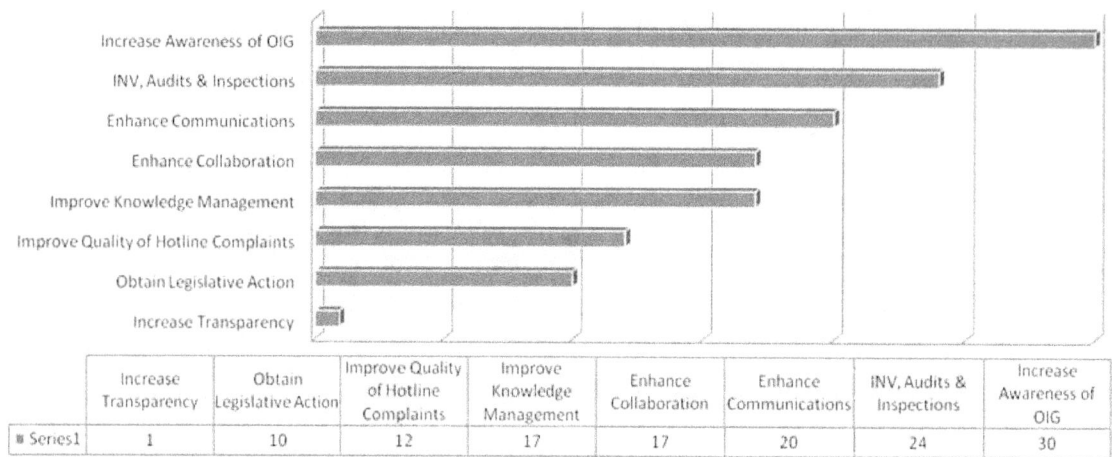

	Increase Transparency	Obtain Legislative Action	Improve Quality of Hotline Complaints	Improve Knowledge Management	Enhance Collaboration	Enhance Communications	INV, Audits & Inspections	Increase Awareness of OIG
▪ Series1	1	10	12	17	17	20	24	30

Figure 4: How New Media Can Serve the OIG Mission

OIGs using new media report that it has improved collaboration efforts and transparency within OIG offices, as well as communication and information sharing both internally and with other agencies. They indicated that new media has increased awareness of the OIG mission, increased interest in OIG audits and investigations, and driven traffic to OIG websites.

Nevertheless, few OIGs have effective metrics in place. Among those that do, some measure work improvements, such as increased collaboration, reduced redundancy in the office, and dollars saved. OIGs using social media tools measure number of postings or retweets and the number of fans, users, or followers (see figure 5).

The Health and Human Services (HHS) OIG recently launched a Most Wanted Fugitives page on its website that allows users to click to report a fugitive. Since coming online in February 2011, this website has generated more than 185,000 visitors, been featured in three congressional testimonies, and been the subject of hundreds of news stories.

OIGs need effective metrics to make appropriate business decisions that consider individual mission needs. Metrics that account for specific new media tools will help OIGs determine the value that new media adds. Such metrics may justify the investment costs, risks, and benefits for certain new media tools and activities, but not necessarily for all. More research and collaboration are needed in this area.

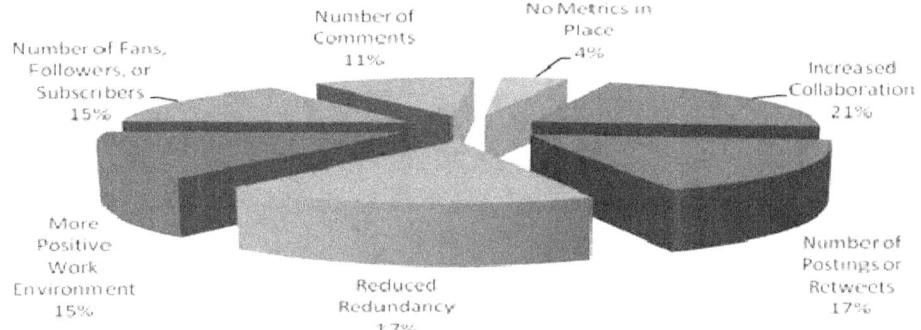

Figure 5: OIG Metrics for New Media

Takeaway

New media can serve the OIG mission in multiple ways, including managing information and knowledge internally, communicating externally, raising awareness of OIG work, increasing the efficiency and effectiveness of OIG personnel, and meeting other mission needs. Although OIGs using new media report positive outcomes, few have the metrics needed to help them make appropriate business decisions.

> *We track the dollars saved by using WebEx to conduct meetings. WebEx savings so far have totaled over $85,000 and 315 staff days in the first half of FY 2011.*
>
> *—OIG survey respondent*

Recommended Practices

We recommend that OIGs using or planning to use new media consider the following practices:

Recommendation #1: Before implementing new media, OIGs should consider how it can serve their particular mission. Factors such as office size, resources, and the programs and operations the OIG oversees will play a role in determining which tools an OIG may want to explore. OIGs interested in implementing new media should consider what other offices have found successful (see appendix B).

Recommendation #2: OIGs should develop effective metrics for new media to help assess the balance of costs, risks, and benefits.

OIGs Are Concerned About Information Security, Privacy Issues, and Legal Oversight

Despite the many ways that new media can serve the OIG mission and the positive experiences that OIGs report, new media presents critical issues that OIGs must confront. Among the concerns that survey respondents reported, issues involving information security, privacy, and legal oversight are the most critical. A recent GAO audit of federal agency use of commercial social media providers stated that "social media technologies present unique challenges and risks, and without establishing guidance and assessing risks specific to social media,

> *A number of organizational constraints (technology, legal, workforce, and FISMA) must be resolved before we can commit to more intense use of new media.*
>
> *—OIG survey respondent*

agencies cannot be assured that they are adequately meeting their responsibilities to manage and preserve federal records, protect the privacy of personal information, and secure federal systems and information against threats."[3] The Working Group discussed these issues at length, but decided that, due to their serious nature, each merited a detailed, individual analysis in follow-up reports. Our main takeaway is that while OIG concerns about information security, privacy, and legal oversight are appropriate and reasonable, they can be managed with the right approach.

Information Security

One of the most critical concerns expressed by OIGs involves information security. OIGs fear that if they embrace certain new media tools, they will expose

> *Our Office of Investigations is concerned about the increased risk of negative exposure due to the lack of protection from viruses and malware, as well as the lack of control of reverse postings to agency message boards.*
>
> *—OIG survey respondent*

their systems to viruses and malware or to another severe threat. Indeed, their worries may be valid; data housed on third-party servers may not receive the protections or assurance of certified and accredited government networks, systems, or personnel. As federal data is stored, processed, and transmitted through unknown and often insecure environments, OIGs may expose themselves to a host of new security, control, and privacy concerns. That said, new media may not present any greater threat to federal data or systems than outside email. Nonetheless, some OIGs choose to block access to certain social media sites or reject certain new media tools.

---

[3] *Federal Agencies Need Policies and Procedures for Managing and Protecting Information They Access and Disseminate* (GAO-11-605), June 2011, highlights summary. This audit report made social media privacy, security, and records retention recommendations to 21 of 23 agencies.

But blocking new media websites is not the easy answer it appears to be. Selective blocking does not eliminate information security threats. The Internet presents unlimited threats, and an OIG cannot realistically block access to all potentially risky sites. Furthermore, with an increasing number of government agencies using new media, at some point an OIG likely will need to review an agency's information security systems. Similarly, with more crimes involving computers and more evidence being found online, investigators will need access to and training on new media tools. As increasing numbers of law enforcement agencies and auditors rely on new media to gather information, an auditor, investigator, or inspector with little or no experience with new media may be handicapped. Blocking access is an easy short-term solution that might diminish investigative and auditing capabilities in the long term. For a brief information security primer, see appendix C.

> *Our organization is relatively small, and the increase in responsibility for creating, updating, and monitoring new media, in addition to related records management, may adversely affect our already limited resources.*
>
> *—OIG survey respondent*

Privacy Issues

Although new media privacy issues may not be the foremost concern to OIGs, they present several potentially serious pitfalls. First, when the government collects personal information from the public, it is required to disclose what kinds of personal information it requires, what it will do with the information, and what purpose the information collection will serve. Collection of personal information via new media is no exception. OIGs need to know what constitutes a collection with respect to new media, what information constitutes personally identifiable information, and when a Privacy Impact Assessment is necessary. Second, new media presents another potential outlet for a privacy breach. OIGs need to ensure that proper privacy controls are in place before, during, and after implementing new media. Such controls may include advising employees through policy and training that disclosure restrictions apply equally to information shared in conversations and on email as to information posted to their personal Facebook accounts or tweeted on Twitter. Finally, OIGs need to ensure that they negotiate terms of service (TOS) agreements with new and social media providers to account for government privacy laws and regulations. Among other things, the TOS agreement should allow the OIG to post its own privacy notice on certain third-party sites. OMB has issued several memoranda on new media privacy issues. See appendix D for a list of legal resources, including these memoranda.

Legal Oversight

OIGs are concerned that legal requirements will overwhelm them as they juggle many issues that may be unfamiliar. Although the General Services Administration (GSA) negotiated TOS agreements with such free social media providers as Facebook, IdeaScale, and YouTube, such agreements are neither one-size-fits-all nor comprehensive. GSA TOS agreements cover the basics, such as amending certain clauses to account for basic federal government requirements and restrictions on such issues as privacy policies, cookies, and jurisdiction; they may not, however, adequately protect every agency's interests. Agency counsel and procurement personnel need to evaluate TOS agreements themselves in light of their particular needs and planned applications. In addition, an OIG needs to know how ethics laws and regulations apply to employee personal use during both duty hours and personal time as well as to employees representing the agency. An OIG also needs to know how to make social media services accessible to the disabled and avoid triggering the *Federal Advisory Committee Act*. Finally, an OIG needs to know how intellectual property law applies to new media. These are only some of the issues that an OIG counsel must address before an office adopts new media.

Concerns About Resources

OIGs question whether investing in new media justifies the resources required. Senior leadership from a number of OIGs, especially the smaller offices, may feel that they lack the funding or staff to create and maintain a robust new media program. Therefore, they are particularly concerned with the benefit-to-cost ratio. New media places demands on OIGs, but the potential costs and risks of not exploring new media may outweigh the cost of required resources. Not understanding and using new media could raise long-term costs, resulting not only in reduced efficiency, but also in less effective oversight. We do not suggest that every OIG adopt an equally robust new media plan. Rather, we suggest that each OIG considering new media conduct its own benefit-to-cost analysis based on its resources and mission needs.

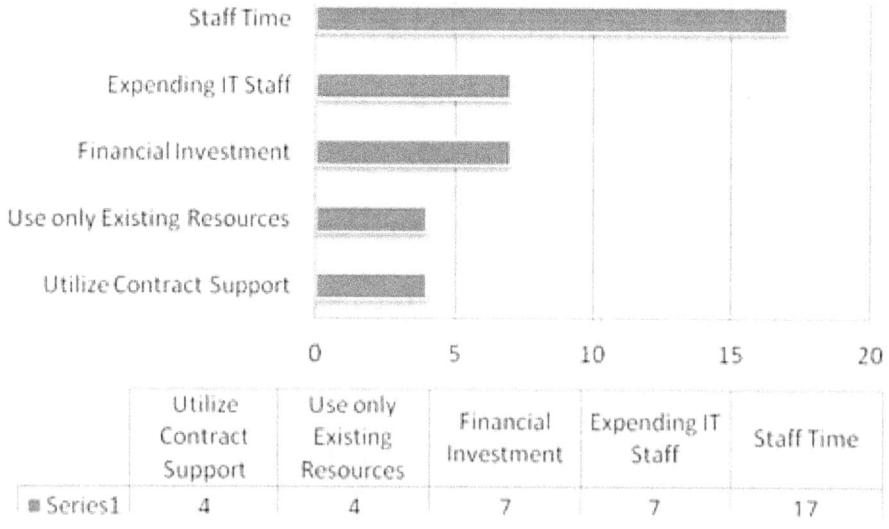

	Utilize Contract Support	Use only Existing Resources	Financial Investment	Expending IT Staff	Staff Time
▪ Series1	4	4	7	7	17

Figure 6: Resources That OIGs Have Expended on New Media

New media does not need to be expensive. Some OIGs report that they do not expend any extra resources. Rather, they use existing resources and free new media tools. Other OIGs, however, spend thousands of dollars on salaries for new media specialists, procurement of expensive technology, and other costs. The most commonly expended resource to develop and manage new media is staff time (see figure 6).

Takeaway

Issues involving information security, privacy, and legal oversight merit serious attention at the outset of any new media efforts. Despite the risks, these issues can be managed successfully with proper planning and the right approach. Lack of resources also prevents some OIGs from implementing new media, but use of the tools need not be expensive. By working together and sharing information, such as on joint efforts like this CIGIE report, the OIG community may ease individual resource constraints, helping smaller OIGs in particular.

Recommended Practice

We recommend that OIGs using or planning to use new media consider the following practices:

Recommendation #3: OIGs should be aware of a multitude of legal and information security issues when employing new media. Before using any new media tool, they should seek input from counsel and information technology (IT) experts, both of whom should continue to be involved throughout implementation. OIGs should consider how new media is being used by both external audiences and employees, since substantial information security investments and policy creation may be necessary to mitigate risks.

Recommendation #4: OIGs should thoroughly assess the potential benefits, costs, and risks in determining whether to use certain new media tools.

New Media Efforts Call for Multidisciplinary Expertise

New media efforts require expertise from many disciplines. Although one person may be responsible for creating or managing content on a public-facing, interactive new media platform, IT personnel, counsel, management, the appropriate program office, and experts in privacy, ethics, procurement, public affairs, and information security should all have input into that content. Experts from just one or two of these areas are unlikely to spot all the issues. New media is a vast field witnessing rapid developments, and responsibility for keeping abreast of changes should be shared.

Several OIGs have created internal working groups or committees to address new media from the planning to implementation stages (see figure 7).

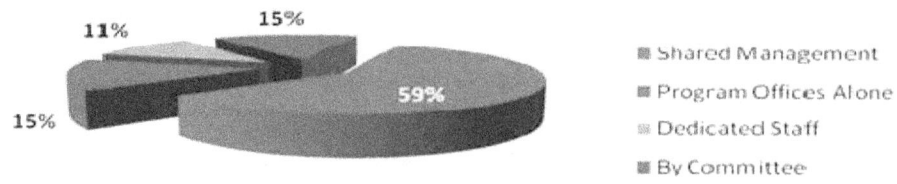

Figure 7: New Media Planning

For example, one survey respondent wrote:

> We established a Web Governance Council, led by the Director of Public Affairs and comprised of representatives from program offices, Executive Office, Counsel, IT, Legislative Affairs, and Management. The purpose of the Council is to serve as a forum for the program offices to provide input on the Web content relating to their work and to suggest ways in which the public affairs office could better highlight that work to the OIG's target audiences.

Sixteen respondents reported that the responsibility for developing and managing the content of the OIG's new media sites was shared across divisions, but not all OIGs involve counsel or IT. Four OIGs reported that program offices alone were responsible for developing and managing content. Failing to involve multidisciplinary expertise exposes an OIG to unnecessary risks.

Takeaway

New media issues transcend offices, professions, and expertise. For this reason, the Working Group included OIG representatives from IT, counsel, public affairs, congressional affairs, management, and inspections. While an OIG should involve counsel and IT experts to ensure that legal and information security issues are considered, other expertise also is needed. The Working Group found that representatives from different professions brought critical knowledge to the table. OIGs involving personnel with a range of expertise are more likely to implement new media successfully while providing reasonable assurance of information security and legal and privacy protections.

Recommended Practice

We recommend that OIGs using or planning to use new media consider the following practice:

Recommendation #5: OIGs interested in using new media should consider involving multiple offices in the effort. The Working Group does not believe that a formal council is necessary, but the Working Group does suggest that agencies involve experts from the following critical areas:

- IT systems/IT security
- Counsel
- Contracting and procurement
- Ethics
- Privacy
- Public affairs
- Congressional affairs
- Program offices
- Management

More Education on New Media Is Needed Within the OIG Community

Survey responses and Working Group discussions revealed a need for more education in new media. First, nearly half of the survey respondents felt that lack of knowledge prevented them from implementing new media to the extent that they wished (see figure 8).

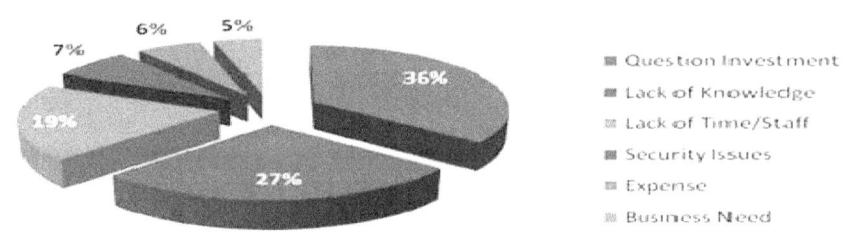

Figure 8: Issues That Prevent OIGs From Implementing New Media

While this report aims to inform and sensitize the OIG community, it is only an initial assessment and can provide neither the comprehensive guidance that OIGs need nor the detailed recommendations that address the specific needs of individual offices. Our survey found that, among other things, OIGs are unclear as to the information security and legal requirements surrounding new media. For example, they are not sure whether or how FISMA applies to new media, or which new media records they are responsible for maintaining. Also, as everyone is aware, new media is dynamic. Established sites such as Facebook introduce new tools and settings on what seems to be a weekly basis, and new tools such as geo-tagging are unveiled one after the other. The new media landscape in a year may look entirely different from that of today, so continuing education will be essential. The points below illustrate the need for more work in this area.

> *The Department of State OIG completed its review of its new media activities in February 2011. The report is available at oig.state.gov/documents/organization/157926.pdf.*

Lack of Oversight

Whether inspired by the Open Government Initiative or acting independently, more and more government agencies are using new media. In response, OIGs will need to address the increasing demand for new media interaction with the agencies they oversee, Congress, and the public.

Most OIGs, however, have not reviewed the new media activities of their agencies, and only a few have plans to do so (see figure 9). This is problematic. First, agencies are operating in an environment in which there is practically no oversight. Given the many serious issues that a government agency must consider, missteps are easy and the consequences are grave. Informed oversight by OIGs is necessary now, and as agencies increase their use of new media, the need will only become greater. Second, OIGs are mandated to review agency programs and operations, but OIGs still appear to lack basic knowledge about new media, severely hampering their oversight efforts. An agency may question an OIG's ability to oversee its new media activities if OIG auditors, investigators, or inspectors themselves are not well versed in new media. In short, OIGs need to be informed about new media issues to monitor agency activities and perform their oversight mission. Continuing education will be essential.

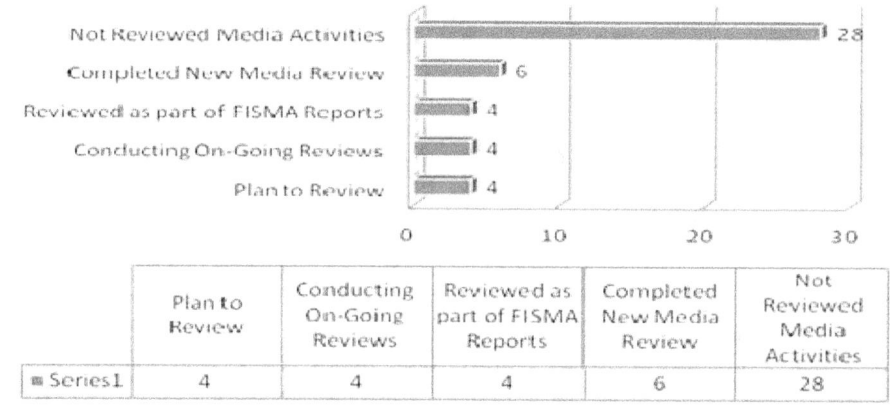

	Plan to Review	Conducting On-Going Reviews	Reviewed as part of FISMA Reports	Completed New Media Review	Not Reviewed Media Activities
Series1	4	4	4	6	28

Figure 9: Review of Agency New Media Activities

> *At its core, new media is about two-way, or interactive, communication. Much of the IG community traditionally has steered away from engaging the public, except in support of its law enforcement mission of preventing and deterring wrongdoing. We are very interested in hearing the experiences of other OIGs that engage in two-way communication using new media.*
>
> *—OIG survey respondent*

FISMA Compliance

OIGs do not agree on whether their new media activities must comply with FISMA. Among other things, FISMA requires that agencies conduct periodic risk assessments[4] and establish appropriate information protection policies based on the harm resulting from unauthorized access, use, disclosure, disruption, modification, or destruction of (1) information collected or maintained by or on behalf of the agency and (2) information systems used or operated by an agency or by a contractor of an agency or other organization on behalf of an agency.[5]

Some respondents reported that they do not consider new media tools to be "major information systems" that require FISMA compliance. Others said that they had not conducted a FISMA review because they were not collecting information from individuals, which would require FISMA compliance. Rather, they were simply using new media to share outbound information, such as posting links to OIG reports, and to repost information that was already public. Some respondents indicated that they thought that FISMA did not apply to specific tools like Twitter or SurveyMonkey, or stated that they were unsure. Regardless of whether OIGs are unsure about FISMA requirements, information security must be considered with all forms of new media. More research and education is essential in this area.

Records Management

To the extent that the use of new media results in the creation of federal records, agencies are responsible for the proper preservation and disposition of those records. Not only may the content of new media be a federal record, but the metadata associated with such content may constitute a federal record as well. Content records include entries, comments, blogs, posts, links, and videos. Repostings of news, information, or other public affairs communications items that are preserved as records elsewhere are not typically considered to be federal record material. Metadata records include information about the content, such as the creator and recipient of the content, date and time of the creation, and receipt of the content.

---

[4] FISMA § 3544(b).
[5] FISMA § 3544.

Our survey found that most OIGs do not have specific records management policies and practices for new media, and consequently do not maintain records of content involving new media. Only one-third of the respondents reported that their recordkeeping policies accounted for new media. Some, however, commented that while their OIG policies were not specific to new media, any new media records fell under their general recordkeeping policies. Some respondents that do not maintain records believe that it is not required because they do not post to external sites. Rather, the content is linked to work products hosted on internal websites or is a copy of records already maintained under applicable records schedules. Because there is considerable confusion about how records management requirements apply to new media, there is a need for more research and education among OIGs, and perhaps an updating of the regulations to provide greater clarity.

Takeaway

OIGs are uncertain about new media requirements regarding information security, FISMA, and records management. Respondents also reported that lack of knowledge prevents them from implementing new media. As a result, the Working Group's most important takeaway for OIGs is that more education is needed. New media has the potential to enhance OIG operations, from the program offices to top management, but OIGs need to know how to comply with information security, privacy, and other legal requirements. Without the necessary knowledge, OIGs may opt to avoid using new media. That choice could negatively affect the oversight mission and prevent OIGs from being as effective as they could be. Lack of oversight could lead to a grave agency misstep, which an IG may be compelled to raise with Congress. In addition, lack of knowledge may result in OIGs using new media inappropriately, agreeing to a contract that does not protect the OIG's interests, or even violating a law or regulation.

The Office of the Inspector General at the Smithsonian Institution is currently conducting an audit of the use of social media at the Smithsonian. Our objectives are to assess whether the Institution's plans for and current uses of social media productively and responsibly advance the Smithsonian mission to increase and diffuse knowledge, including whether the Institution provides adequate oversight and sufficient accountability. We initiated the audit to address the risk posed by users posting inappropriate content on Smithsonian accounts. We also undertook the audit because the Smithsonian's Strategic Plan emphasized the importance of these tools in advancing the Institution's mission, and we were concerned that the Smithsonian ensure adequate oversight of and accountability for social media use. We expect to issue a final report not later than September 30, 2011.

The Working Group learned firsthand how important education is to understanding new media's potential for rewards and risks. Members' experiences with new media varied at the beginning of our discussions. Several brought specialized experience in new media, while others were not familiar with such common tools as Facebook or SharePoint. In the end, however, all members learned a great deal about individual new media tools, current and prospective OIG use of them, and the risks involved. Without that shared education, Working Group members would not be in a position to advise their agency leadership on strategy or identify several recommended practices in this report.

The Working Group believes that OIGs involved with new media need to undergo a similarly rigorous assessment. Taking into consideration survey comments and responses, we suggest that OIGs work together, under the auspices of CIGIE, to share knowledge and experiences. Individual OIG new media needs may differ, but OIGs confront similar business, legal, and security issues. By sharing experiences, OIGs can avoid having to start individually from scratch and, at the same time, collectively ensure greater efficiency in meeting their common oversight mission.

Finally, new media is dynamic. OIGs need to be aware of ongoing changes, not only to ensure that their own new media use will be current but also to oversee their agencies effectively.

Recommended Practice

We recommend that OIGs using or planning to use new media consider the following practice:

Recommendation #6: OIGs should offer and encourage training to all personnel involved in new media activities, whether as part of the OIG's new media use or for purposes of oversight of the agency. For maximum efficiency, CIGIE may facilitate such training with the help of the Working Group.

> *As commercial, web-based social media technologies and new media activities are a relatively new function or resource available to our agency and the OIG, very little internal policy or guidance has been developed or published regarding these activities, including information related to records retention, authority to post, and so forth.*
>
> *—OIG survey respondent*

Conclusion, Proposed Areas for Further Study, and Recommendation to CIGIE

OIGs recognize that new media is here for the long term, and some have advanced quite far in establishing their own capabilities. Others have adopted a wait-and-see posture, due at least in part to uncertainty about the benefits and risks. Whether an OIG's focus is on monitoring its agency's new media use, implementing its own new media program, or both, the Working Group hopes that this report will serve to inform and inspire.

Most of the work still lies ahead, however. Survey results revealed disagreement among OIGs regarding critical aspects of new media use, such as the legal requirements involving FISMA, record keeping, and privacy issues. There were other surprising results in the survey, such as that some OIGs do not involve IT experts, counsel, or public affairs in their new media efforts. In addition, this report is being released at a time when many OIGs are in the midst of planning and developing new capabilities. The survey results showed that in the near future, 13 OIGs identified as non-media users expect to begin implementing new media. Thirty-one OIGs may soon launch Facebook or Twitter accounts, and several OIGs will finish reviewing their agencies' new media activities. Finally, OIGs responding to the survey expressed the desire to see the OIG community work together on new media to share information, learn from each other's experiences, and improve knowledge management. As one respondent said,

> The IG community has accumulated a large amount of institutional knowledge over the years. As in most similar groups, this knowledge is not always well organized or managed. We have over 60 different silos, with relatively little sharing among IGs. Further, even inside the silos, knowledge management is not what it could be.

Given these concerns, the Working Group proposes that CIGIE establish a permanent group to function as an information-sharing and training resource for CIGIE and individual OIGs.

Recommendation to CIGIE: Amid a rapidly changing and demanding environment, the Working Group suggests that CIGIE establish a permanent standing working group focused on emerging technologies and their impact on the OIG community. Such a working group would leverage knowledge and experience, and help ease individual resource constraints. The working group would:

- Develop a CIGIE training course for OIG personnel on new media issues. Such training should be offered to OIG leadership, management, auditors, investigators, inspectors, evaluators, counsel, ethics officials, procurement officials, public affairs, and IT staff.

- Organize a new media conference for the OIG community consisting of panels covering the myriad issues reviewed in this report, and participate in and contribute to the annual Government Web and New Media Conference.

- Continue to research and discuss emerging technologies, in particular how the government is leveraging them and how such use may affect the OIG community.

- Issue educational guides on critical issues in new media, including the following:
  - Information security
  - Legal issues
  - Privacy issues

Summary: Recommended Practices to OIGs

We recommend that OIGs using or planning to use new media consider the following practices:

Recommendation #1: Before implementing new media, OIGs should consider how it can serve their particular mission. Factors such as office size, resources, and the programs and operations the OIG oversees will play a role in determining which tools an OIG may want to explore. OIGs interested in implementing new media should consider what other offices have found successful (see appendix B).

Recommendation #2: OIGs should develop effective metrics for new media to help assess the balance of costs, risks, and benefits.

Recommendation #3: OIGs should be aware of a multitude of legal and information security issues when employing new media. Before using any new media tool, they should seek input from counsel and IT experts, both of whom should continue to be involved throughout implementation. OIGs should consider how new media is being used by both external audiences and employees, since substantial information security investments and policy creation may be necessary to mitigate risks.

Recommendation #4: OIGs should thoroughly assess the potential benefits, costs, and risks in determining whether to use certain new media tools.

Recommendation #5: OIGs interested in using new media should consider involving multiple offices in the effort. The Working Group does not believe that a formal council is necessary, but it does suggest that agencies involve experts from the following critical areas:

- IT systems/IT security
- Counsel

- Contracting and procurement
- Ethics
- Privacy
- Public affairs
- Congressional affairs
- Program offices
- Management

Recommendation #6: OIGs should offer and encourage training to all personnel involved in new media activities, whether as part of the OIG's new media use or for purposes of oversight of the agency. For maximum efficiency, CIGIE may facilitate such training with the help of the Working Group.

We undertook this review at the request of CIGIE's Homeland Security Roundtable. The purpose of this review was to sensitize OIGs to the ways new media can be used to further the mission and goals of an OIG. In addition, we sought to address why an OIG needs to be aware of new media developments, particularly how new media may affect an OIG's oversight responsibilities.

This report makes six recommendations to OIGs and one recommendation to CIGIE. The report is not, however, a comprehensive analysis of all the legal, privacy, policy, and security-related issues associated with the use of new media; it is a baseline assessment. In addition, the new media tools and technologies identified in this report are not an endorsement of any commercial products, services, or entities.

The Working Group was staffed with public affairs specialists, attorneys, IT professionals, and other subject matter experts and included representatives of presidentially appointed and designated federal entity Inspectors General. We met regularly from December 2010 until the date of this publication. At the outset, we sent a questionnaire to OIGs represented at the Working Group. The Working Group then formulated and administered a survey to the 79 CIGIE members to seek input on their experiences with and views on new media. This report is based on a review of survey responses from 39 OIGs, the subject matter expertise of new media specialists, discussions with industry professionals, legal research, and a review of applicable documents.

The list of OIGs that use the tools in this appendix reflects OIGs that responded to the survey and agreed to be contacted; it may not be exhaustive.

Blogs
An easy-to-update website or webpage where bloggers write entries in a diary-like format. Some also allow readers to engage in conversations with the blogger and other readers.

- **Department of Commerce:** To promote internal communications in the OIG. Written and video blogs are created on the OIG intranet with posts written by the senior staff and the IG.

Facebook
A social networking website that connects people and allows OIG users to find people they know among other members, look for members with similar interests or affiliations, and establish networks of contacts.

- **Department of Education (ED):** To reach a large audience with information on the OIG's mission and efforts, attract potential new staff, and encourage those involved in education to aid in identifying waste, fraud, and abuse. Information uploaded onto Facebook is automatically updated to Twitter, and the OIG responds to comments posted by the public. All OIG posts direct traffic to the OIG's website for new reports, job vacancies, and so on.
- **NASA:** To update Congress, NASA, the GAO, the media, the public, and the IG community about the release of OIG reports and other items of interest, including new projects, letters to Congress, NASA's management challenges, press releases, and Semi-Annual Reports. Facebook provides a timely and concise vehicle for distributing information about the OIG mission, products, activities, and significant accomplishments, and allows users easy and direct access to a wide variety of OIG information, while providing an avenue for public comments.

LinkedIn
A business-oriented networking site to establish connections, announce or search for jobs, create personal profiles, and expand professional contacts.

- **Treasury Inspector General for Tax Administration (TIGTA):** To facilitate recruiting and increase awareness of the OIG.
- **U.S. Capitol Police:** To increase awareness of the OIG.

OMB Max
A federal government cloud that allows government employees and contractors to share information and collaborate in an easy, secure, and comprehensive interface. Users can post documents, restrict access to designated groups or users, solicit comments, edit materials, publish briefing books and other data, contribute to a "wiki," and participate in meetings from a remote location.

- **Farm Credit Administration (FCA):** To complete the OIG section of the FISMA report.
- **Department of Health and Human Services (HHS):** To share information.
- **TIGTA:** To facilitate information sharing.
- **U.S. Railroad Retirement Board (RRB):** To obtain and share information. OMB Max has become OMB's primary means of communicating with agencies.
- **Peace Corps:** To facilitate FISMA reporting.
- **Office of Personnel Management (OPM):** To provide FISMA audit documentation and information on OPM's claims data warehouse project.
- **U.S. Department of Veterans Affairs (VA):** To obtain SF 133 and SF 132 reports and ad hoc OMB guidance.

RSS Feed
News feeds that allow the OIG to alert users to new content or updates on its website. The alerts, which are delivered directly to the users, usually include article summaries to help the users decide whether to go to the website for more information.

- **Corporation for National and Community Service (CNCS):** To promote new reports on the OIG's website.
- **Department of Transportation (DOT):** To promote newly released reports and drive traffic to the OIG website.
- **HHS:** To disseminate information to stakeholders/general public about the OIG and its work.
- **U.S. Agency for International Development (USAID):** To announce reports and press releases in a way that makes them easily accessible to the public, congressional staff, and other stakeholders at low cost.
- **RRB:** To promote newly released reports.
- **VA:** To allow visitors to the OIG's external website to receive subscriptions to specific categories of published content, such as reports by type, monthly highlights, press releases, or congressional testimony.
- **U.S. Capitol Police:** To increase awareness of the OIG.
- **State Department:** To reach audiences and drive traffic to the OIG Website. The department manages the RSS feed application.
- **Federal Trade Commission:** To increase awareness of the OIG and announce publicly available audit reports.
- **Department of Commerce:** To increase awareness of the OIG. The RSS feed is on the OIG's website and has received positive feedback from stakeholders.

SharePoint
Widely used software that enables internal web portals for document sharing and search, team collaboration, blogs, wikis, and distributing news to those granted access.

- **TIGTA:** To provide employees with historical information, training, policy and guidance, and links to useful tools. The software also helps the OIG manage and coordinate special program initiatives; maintain case summaries; and remotely manage, share, collaborate, and communicate information among field divisions and headquarters.

- **DOT:** To share internal information among employees and create external awareness of the results of OIG audits and investigations.
- **Department of Labor (DOL):** To enhance communication and collaboration among employees.
- **United States International Trade Commission (USITC):** To promote internal communications among employees and improve collaboration and knowledge management within the OIG.
- **HHS:** To assist teams across the OIG in producing publications and reports.
- **National Science Foundation (NSF):** To provide an internal site for sharing documents, policies, and links to useful websites. Also used for reserving conference rooms and announcing meetings and events.
- **VA:** To provide a collaborative tool for end users, store documents for collaboration, and provide a location for policies and procedures. SharePoint has been the OIG's intranet backbone since 2007, and the office recently formed a SharePoint users' group to explore additional uses.
- **U.S. Department of Agriculture:** To reach existing employees and facilitate dialogue among staff.
- **U.S. Capitol Police:** To share information internally.
- **Small Business Administration (SBA):** To share and collaborate on documents, reports, and policies.
- **State Department:** To promote internal communication among employees. OIG manages its own SharePoint site.

Survey tools (e.g., SurveyMonkey)

Online survey tools that enable users to create their own web-based surveys. May be used internally and externally.

- **Peace Corps:** To solicit stakeholder feedback on the OIG's evaluation reports once they are released.
- **DOL:** To gather data.
- **TIGTA:** To obtain information for use in audits.
- **VA:** To conduct customer satisfaction surveys after the issuance of each audit and inspection, and to conduct internal staff surveys.
- **U.S. Capitol Police:** To collect information in furtherance of our mission.
- **SBA:** To seek employee ideas and feedback on internal communications, strategy, policy, and other topics. SurveyMonkey allows anonymous responses, when needed.
- **OPM:** To receive feedback on internal investigations, meetings, and so on.
- **Tennessee Valley Authority (TVA):** To conduct internal surveys.
- **Environmental Protection Agency:** To conduct internal surveys.

Twitter

A service that enables users to write up to 140-character blog posts and follow others who "tweet." The messages, which can be read online or via a cell phone or other mobile device, are used for dispensing news and making announcements, obtaining feedback on new ideas, establishing a network of people, and obtaining information that may be useful for audits and investigations.

- **CNCS**: To get news out instantly to a wide audience when releasing a new report on the OIG's website, closing out a case, or making other official announcements. Most followers are CNCS stakeholders, precisely the group the OIG is trying to reach. Twitter has increased traffic to its website and replaced the old electronic mailing list.
- **DOT:** To distribute reports by a method that is simple and uses minimal resources.
- **HHS:** To reach audiences in the health care, compliance, and provider communities and amplify the impact of the OIG's work. One journalist tweeted a link to the OIG's Twitter site to his 1,000 followers, suggesting that they follow the HHS OIG site.
- **ED:** To reach new audiences with information on the OIG's mission and efforts, attract potential new staff, and encourage those involved in education to aid in identifying waste, fraud, and abuse. Twitter is simple to use and provides a good way to distribute reports. Information uploaded onto Facebook is automatically updated to Twitter, and the OIG responds to comments posted by the public. All OIG posts direct traffic to the OIG's website for new reports, job vacancies, and so on.
- **NASA:** To provide Congress, NASA, the GAO, the media, the public, and the IG community with timely updates on OIG products without searching the Web, Twitter supplies NASA OIG followers with updates on a variety of issues in a concise and easily accessible format. NASA OIG tweets new projects, letters, and reports to Congress, NASA's management challenges, and press releases.
- **OPM:** To obtain information on persons of interest.
- **State Department:** To reach audiences and drive traffic to the OIG website. Since OIG created a Twitter account, visits to the OIG website and the accessing of posted reports have increased. Twitter also provides information for use in audits, investigations, inspections, and evaluations. OIG manages its own Twitter account while adhering to department guidelines.
- **National Labor Relations Board (NLRB):** To promote newly released reports and communicate about the OIG's work.

WebEx

Applications that provide on-demand collaboration, online meeting, web conferencing, and video conferencing capabilities.

- **TIGTA:** To facilitate collaborative meetings, remote participation by teleworkers in meetings, and training, with substantial savings in staff time and travel costs.

- **OPM:** To enable remote collaboration, presentations, training, meetings, and desktop sharing.

Wiki

A collaborative workspace on the Web that allows users to contribute or edit content and develop documents or web pages. Access to wikis can be public, where anyone can see the content, or limited to a defined community within or across organizations. The Council of Counsels to the Inspectors General maintains a wiki on OMB Max.

- **USAID:** To improve knowledge management inside the designated community.
- **U.S. Capitol Police:** To increase awareness of the OIG.
- **State Department:** To conduct general and specialized searches of the department's and individual bureaus' internal websites using the wiki-based site Diplopedia. The department manages this wiki; OIG provides input only to its own Diplopedia entries.
- **TVA:** To enhance communication among OIG employees, the OIG created an internal Wiki.

YouTube

A video-sharing website that allows users to upload and share user-generated video content, including movie clips, television clips, and music videos, as well as amateur content.

- **HHS:** To educate and inform stakeholders and the public about the OIG mission.

New media, including social media, often appears to confound the traditional security model for federal agencies. Traditionally, agencies control all aspects of an information system or contracted information services. Since many new media applications are free, they can be accessed outside of the authority of an agency's Chief Information Officer (CIO). Among other things, CIOs are responsible for providing for the development and maintenance of minimum controls required to protect federal information and information systems used by or on behalf of agencies. More attention has been given to the protection of information systems, as most federal data reside on internal agency networks, and these systems are tangible, traceable assets.

In contrast to the practice with traditional internal agency networks, some federal data will no longer be maintained on internal systems as agencies increasingly utilize new media tools. Therefore, the data may not receive the protections or assurance of certified and accredited government networks. As federal data is stored, processed, and transmitted through unknown and often insecure environments, agencies may expose themselves to a host of new security and privacy concerns that will need to be addressed. Internal and external demand for access to new media websites, "apps," and other digital services also puts pressure on agencies to permit access through secure government networks. In addition, the popularity of new media sites makes them attractive targets for malicious activities and actors. Many organizations and businesses block new media sites for a variety of reasons, including security, privacy, and network performance issues. Including the CIO, information security officer, privacy official, counsel, public affairs, and other stakeholders in the planning can greatly decrease the legal, reputational, and financial risks of using social media and new media services. When an agency determines that access to new media through secure government networks is appropriate, additional safeguards and risk acceptance or mitigation should be considered. Such safeguards include, but are not limited to, applying FISMA and engaging with new media providers.

Federal Information Security Management Act

Whether FISMA applies to new media has emerged as a debatable and sometimes contentious issue because of ever-changing nomenclature and dearth of official federal guidance. New media is often defined by the name of a specific tool, company, service, or application. At this time, however, there is little official guidance that identifies, defines, and unites these tools. As a result, efforts to address them are often as fractured as the terms used within the organization. Agencies should carefully consider the impact FISMA may have on new media adoption.

Engagement With New Media Providers

When utilizing new media and social media services, agencies must consider additional risk management. Service providers may or may not be willing to enter into a contract with specific terms of service addressing security, privacy, and other concerns. If the vendor is not willing to negotiate and the terms as provided could result in unacceptable risks or additional costs, the agency should reconsider its options. Agencies should carefully review and negotiate contracts with new media providers to ensure that appropriate security, privacy, and other matters are clearly defined and meet federal government requirements.

The following table lists various laws, regulations, guidance, and other legal resources that an OIG may find useful in creating and maintaining its new media program. However, it is not meant to be a comprehensive or exhaustive list, and each OIG should consider its own needs and requirements in determining which laws, regulations, and guidance are applicable to its specific situation.

Area of Interest	Applicable Statutes, Regulations, and Guidance	Description
Ethics	5 C.F.R. § 2635.702	No endorsements of any product, service, or enterprise
	5 C.F.R. § 2635.703	Employees may not use nonpublic information to further private interest or that of another
	5 C.F.R. § 2635.703(b)	Employees may not disclose nonpublic information
	5 C.F.R. § 2635.704	Duty to protect and not use government property (de minimus exception)
	5 C.F.R. § 2635.705	Duty to use official time to perform official duties
	5 C.F.R. § 2635.801 et seq; 18 U.S.C. § 203(a); 18 U.S.C. § 209; 5 C.F.R. § 2636.305, et seq.	Restrictions on outside employment and nongovernmental activities
	41 U.S.C. § 423	Restrictions on disclosing and obtaining contractor bid or proposal information or source selection information
Procurement & Terms of Service	*Clinger-Cohen Act of 1996*, 40 U.S.C. § 1401(3)	Establishes a comprehensive approach for executive agencies to improve the acquisition and management of their information resources
	48 C.F.R. § 6.101	Requires full and open competition
	48 C.F.R. § 4.101	Allows only contracting officers to sign contracts on behalf of the United States
Information Collection, Management, & Privacy	*Privacy Act of 1974*, 5 U.S.C. § 552(a), as amended	Governs the collection, maintenance, use, and dissemination of information about individuals that is maintained in systems of records by federal agencies
	Procurement Integrity Act, 41 U.S.C. § 423, implemented at FAR 3.104	Prohibits the release of source selection and contractor bid or proposal information
	Freedom of Information Act, 5 U.S.C. § 552(a), as amended	Gives the public the right to request access to records of the executive branch of the government unless the information is protected from disclosure
	Executive Order 13526, Classified National Security Information	Prescribes a uniform system for classifying, safeguarding, and declassifying national security information

Area of Interest	Applicable Statutes, Regulations, and Guidance	Description
	E-government Act of 2002, 44 U.S.C. § 101	Promotes the use of the Internet to make the federal government more transparent
	18 U.S.C. § 1905	Prohibits disclosure of proprietary information and certain other information of a confidential nature
	Policies for Federal Agency Public Websites, OMB Memorandum M-05-04	Requires agencies to manage public websites as part of their information resource management program and to be in compliance with federal information resource management law and policy
	Safeguarding Personally Identifiable Information, OMB Memorandum M-06-15	Requires that a review be conducted to address all administrative, technical, and physical means used to ensure privacy of personally identifiable information
	Protection of Sensitive Agency Information, OMB Memorandum M-06-16	Provides a security checklist and recommends other actions to be taken to protect sensitive agency information
	Reporting Incidents Involving Personally Identifiable Information and Incorporating the Cost for Security in Agency Information Technology Investments, OMB Memorandum M-06-19	Provides updated guidance on the reporting of security incidents involving personally identifiable information
	Safeguarding Against and Responding to the Breach of Personally Identifiable Information, OMB Memorandum M-07-16	Requires agencies to develop and implement a breach notification policy and provides the framework within which agencies must develop the policy while ensuring that proper safeguards are in place to protect the information
	Privacy Policies on Federal Web Sites, OMB Memorandum M-99-18	Directs departments and agencies to post clear privacy policies on websites and provides guidance for doing so

Area of Interest	Applicable Statutes, Regulations, and Guidance	Description
	Guidance for Agency Use of Third-Party Websites and Applications, OMB Memorandum M-10-23	Provides guidance to federal agencies on how to protect privacy, consistent with the law, while using third-party Web-based technologies
	Guidance for Online Use of Web Measurement and Customization Technologies, OMB Memorandum M-10-22	Provides guidance for using customization technologies (i.e., cookies); requires that users be notified and allowed to opt out
	Government Paperwork Elimination Act, Pub. L. No. 105-277	Requires federal agencies to allow individuals or entities that deal with the agencies the option to submit information or transact with the agency electronically, when practicable, and to main records electronically, when practicable
	Paperwork Reduction Act, 44 U.S.C. § 3501 et. seq.	Establishes a process whereby OMB reviews and approves plans to collect information from the public where there are 10 or more participants
	Social Media, Interactive Technologies and the Paperwork Reduction Act, OMB Office of Information and Regulatory Affairs Memorandum, April 7, 2010	Explains that the *Paperwork Reduction Act* does not apply to many uses of social media and technologies
Information Quality	*Information Quality Act*, Pub. L. No. 105-554, § 515	Requires that federal agencies follow guidelines that ensure and maximize the quality, objectivity, utility, and integrity of information they disseminate
	Guidelines for Ensuring and Maximizing the Quality, Objectivity, Utility, and Integrity of Information Disseminated by Federal Agencies (Republication), 67 Fed. Reg. 8452	OMB guidance on implementing the *Information Quality Act*
	Plain Language Act, Pub. L. No. 111-274	Requires the federal government to write all new publications, forms, and publicly distributed documents in a "clear, concise, well-organized" manner

Area of Interest	Applicable Statutes, Regulations, and Guidance	Description
	Final Guidance on Implementing the Plain Writing Act of 2010, OMB Memorandum M-11-15	Provides guidance on implementing the plain writing requirements of the *Plain Writing Act of 2010*
Information Security	*Federal Information Security Management Act of 2002*, 44 U.S.C. § 3541, et. seq.	Requires each federal agency to develop, document, and implement an agency-wide program to provide information security for the information and information systems that support the operations and assets of the agency
	New FISMA Privacy Reporting Requirements for FY 2008, OMB Memorandum M-08-09	Provides advance notice about new FISMA reporting requirements, mostly regarding privacy reviews and privacy issues
	Guidelines on Securing Public Web Servers, NIST Special Publication 800-44	Provides guidance on implementing appropriate security management practices and controls when maintaining and operating a secure Web server
	FY 2004 Reporting Instructions for the Federal Information Security Management Act, OMB Memorandum M-04-25	Provides guidance and instructions to agencies on how to implement the requirements of FISMA and how to report to OMB and Congress on the effectiveness of their security programs
Accessibility	Section 508 Amendment to the *Rehabilitation Act of 1973*, Pub. L. No. 105-220, § 508	Requires that all website content be equally accessible to people with disabilities applies to Web applications, Web pages, all attached files, intranet sites, and public-facing Web pages
	Improving Access to Services for Persons with Limited English Proficiency, Executive Order No. 13,166	Requires federal agencies to provide meaningful access to those with limited English proficiency
	Improving Public Access to and Dissemination of Government Information and Using the Federal Enterprise Architecture Data Reference Model, OMB Memorandum M-06-02	Identifies procedures to organize and categorize information and make it searchable across agencies to improve public access and dissemination

Area of Interest	Applicable Statutes, Regulations, and Guidance	Description
Records Management	*Federal Records Act*, 44 U.S.C. Chapters 21, 29, 31 & 33	44 U.S.C. Chapter 21 National Archives and Records Administration 44 U.S.C. Chapter 29 Records Management by the Archivist of the United States and by the Administrator of General Services 44 U.S.C. Chapter 31 Records Management by Federal Agencies 44 U.S.C. Chapter 33 Disposal of Records
	Records Management, 36 C.F.R. Chapter XII, Subchapter B	Regulations regarding the creation, maintenance and disposition of various types of records. Part 1234 applies to electronic records management.
	Management of Federal Information Resources, OMB Circular A-130	Provides uniform government-wide information resources management policies as required by the *Paperwork Reduction Act of 1980*
	Guidance on Managing Records in Cloud Computing Environments, NARA Bulletin 2010-05	Addresses records management considerations in cloud computing environments and is the formal articulation of NARA's view of agencies' records management responsibilities.
	NARA Guidance on Managing Web Records, January 2005	Guidance to assist agency officials in mitigating the risks an agency faces by using the Web to carry out agency business
	Implications of Recent Web Technologies for NARA Web Guidance	Explores some Web applications and their impact on records management
	NARA Guidance on Managing Records in Web 2.0/Social Media Platforms, NARA Bull. 2011-02	Provides guidance on managing records produced when federal agencies use Web 2.0/social media platforms for federal business
Intellectual Property	*Lanham Act*, 15 U.S.C. §§ 1051, et seq.	Provides for a national system of trademark registration and protects the owner of a federally registered mark against use of similar marks
	Anticybersquatting Consumer Protection Act, 15 U.S.C. § 1125(d)	Establishes a cause of action for registering, trafficking in, or using a domain name confusingly similar to, or dilutive of, a trademark or personal name

Area of Interest	Applicable Statutes, Regulations, and Guidance	Description
	Uniform Domain Name Dispute Resolution Policy	A process established by the Internet Corporation for Assigned Names and Numbers to resolve disputes regarding domain names
	Digital Millennium Copyright Act, Pub. L. No. 105-304	Provides heightened penalties for copyright infringement on the Internet
	Use of Department Seals, 18 U.S.C. §§ 508, 1017	Prohibits the wrongful use of seals of departments and agencies
	Use of US Government Seals, 18 U.S.C. § 713	Prohibits the wrongful use of seals of the United States, the President, the Vice President, and Congress
Politics	Lobbying with Appropriated Moneys, 18 U.S.C. § 1913	Prohibits the use of appropriated funds to lobby member of Congress
	Hatch Act, 5 §§ U.S.C. 7321-7326	Governs the participation by certain federal executive branch employees in partisan political management or partisan political campaigns
	Political Activities of Federal Employees, 5 C.F.R. § 734	Regulations implementing the *Hatch Act*
Advisory Committees	*Federal Advisory Committee Act*, 5 U.S.C. Appendix 2	Governs the behavior of federal advisory committees by restricting their formation, limiting their powers, and limiting the length of time committees may operate. Also declares that all administrative procedures and hearings are to be public knowledge.
First Amendment	5 U.S.C. § 552a(e)(7)	Prohibits maintaining records on how individuals exercise First Amendment rights

Section 1: Introduction

The CIGIE New Media Working Group seeks your participation and input about the current state of new media use in the Inspector General community, including information about best practices and possible areas of concern. The results of this survey will assist the CIGIE New Media Working Group in developing non-binding guidance on the potential uses of new media in the Inspector General community.

As you respond to the survey questions, please keep in mind that "new media" is much more than social media tools such as Twitter, Facebook, and LinkedIn, with which you may be more familiar. Rather, new media encompasses all forms of electronic and interactive media, which can dramatically enhance internal, intra-governmental and external interactions and knowledge management. To cite some examples, OMB Max facilitates information sharing, collaboration, data collection, analytics, and publishing activities in a FISMA-compliant, government cloud. Other tools facilitate surveys, project management, and mind mapping. For your information, a glossary of terms describing the new media tools referenced in this survey is enclosed as an attachment to the accompanying email.

Section 2: Demographic Information

1. **Please identify which Office of Inspector General (OIG) you represent.**

2. **Whom may we contact if we have questions regarding your answers? Please provide name, phone number and email address.**

3. **Does your OIG currently use new media?**
   ☐ Yes
   ☐ No, but we are considering using new media.

   Comments:

Section 3: General Questions About The OIG Community And New Media

1. **How would your OIG like to see new media serve the IG mission? Please check all responses that apply.**

   ☐ Enhancing collaboration and knowledge management within the OIG community.
   ☐ Improving quality of hotline complaints.
   ☐ Obtaining comments and feedback that may increase the OIG's ability to provide effective oversight.
   ☐ Increasing the likelihood of obtaining agency or legislative action on OIG recommendations.
   ☐ Improving collaboration and knowledge management within your OIG.

□ Increasing awareness of OIG.
□ Helping auditors, investigators and evaluators perform their respective jobs.
□ Recruiting
□ Enhancing communications among OIG employees.
□ Other: (Please specify)

2. What prevents your OIG from using new media?

□ Lack of time.
□ It's an issue of investment vs. resources.
□ Lack of knowledge.
□ Increased expense.
□ Other. (Please specify)

3. Has your OIG reviewed the new media activities of the agency you oversee? If yes, please provide a link to the report.

□ We are planning one.
□ Yes, as part of a FISMA report on compliance with OMB A-130.
□ Ongoing.
□ No.

Please provide a link to any relevant reports along with any other comments you may have.

Section 4: Considering The Use of New Media

1. What type of new media is your OIG considering using for internal and/or external use? Please check all that apply.

□ Audio or video podcasts.
□ LinkedIn
□ Knowledge management tools.
□ SharePoint.
□ Survey tools such as SurveyMonkey.
□ Blogs.
□ RSS Feed.
□ Twitter.
□ YouTube.
□ Wikipedia.
□ IdeaScale.
□ Facebook.
□ OMB Max.
□ Other: (Please specify and add any comments you may have.)

2. **If your OIG is considering the use of new media, which offices are involved in the planning? Please check all that apply.**

☐ Program offices (Audit, Investigations, Inspections/Evaluations, etc.).
☐ Human Resources.
☐ Information Technology.
☐ Communications/Public Affairs/External Affairs.
☐ Counsel.
☐ Other: (Please specify)

Section 5: OIGs That Currently Use New Media

Please fill out this section if your OIG currently uses new media.

1. **How is your OIG using new media (either internally or externally)? Please check all that apply.**

☐ To promote newly released reports.
☐ For knowledge management purposes
☐ To facilitate dialogue with stakeholders
☐ To facilitate dialogue with the general public
☐ To comply with the Open Government initiative to increase transparency and collaboration with the general public.
☐ To reach potential employees
☐ To drive traffic to the OIG website
☐ To reach existing employees.
☐ To promote internal communication among employees.
☐ To obtain information for use in audits, investigations, inspections or evaluations.
☐ Other (please specify or provide any comments you may have).

2. **Which new media products does your OIG use? Please check all that apply.**

☐ OMB Max.
☐ Knowledge management tools
☐ Blogs
☐ IdeaScale
☐ Wikipedia
☐ LinkedIn
☐ Facebook
☐ Twitter
☐ YouTube.
☐ Survey tools such as SurveyMonkey.
☐ Sharepoint.
☐ Audio or video podcasts.

    ☐ RSS Feed.

    ☐ Other (please specify or provide any comments you may have.

3. **Please describe your OIG's overall experiences with new media.**

4. **What resources has your OIG expended so far to set up and manage your new media activities?**

5. **Which offices in your OIG have responsibility for developing and management content for your OIG's new media sites? For each office, please indicate the number of hours devoted to new media activity each week.**

Counsel
☐ None
☐ Less than 5 hours
☐ Less than 10 hours
☐ Less than 15 hours
☐ Less than 20 hours
☐ Less than 30 hours
☐ Full-time

Information Technology
☐ None
☐ Less than 5 hours
☐ Less than 10 hours
☐ Less than 15 hours
☐ Less than 20 hours
☐ Less than 30 hours
☐ Full-time

Program Offices: (Audit, Investigations, Investigations, etc.)
☐ None
☐ Less than 5 hours
☐ Less than 10 hours
☐ Less than 15 hours
☐ Less than 20 hours
☐ Less than 30 hours
☐ Full-time

Public Affairs/External Relations/Communications
☐ None
☐ Less than 5 hours
☐ Less than 10 hours
☐ Less than 15 hours

☐ Less than 20 hours
☐ Less than 30 hours
☐ Full-time

Shared responsibility
☐ None
☐ Less than 5 hours
☐ Less than 10 hours
☐ Less than 15 hours
☐ Less than 20 hours
☐ Less than 30 hours
☐ Full-time

Other (please specify and add any comments you may have.)

6. **Are your new media activities FISMA-compliant? Please explain why or why not.**

☐ Yes
☐ No

Please provide additional information regarding your answer.

7. **Do you maintain records of content posted on external news sites?**

☐ Yes
☐ No

Comments:

8. **Does your OIG have a policy or practices regarding record keeping of new media activities?**

☐ Yes
☐ No

Please elaborate on your answer and indicate whether you would be willing to share a copy of your policy.

9. **What is your OIG's measure of the effectiveness of your new media use? Please check all that apply.**

☐ Dollars saved
☐ More assets recovered
☐ Number of postings or retweets
☐ More positive work environment.

☐ Number of comments
☐ More effective audits
☐ Number of users, fans, followers or subscribers
☐ Increased collaboration.
☐ More effective investigations.
☐ Reduced redundant work; greater efficiency.
☐ Other: (Please specify and provide examples.)

Section 6: OIGs That Use Twitter

Please fill out this section if your OIG uses Twitter.

1. **Why does your OIG use Twitter?**

☐ Good way to distribute reports.
☐ Large number of users.
☐ Most closely aligned with our current capabilities.
☐ Least use of resources.
☐ It provides us with information for use in audits, investigations, inspections and evaluations.
☐ Simplicity of use.
☐ Other: (Please specify.)

2. **Do you screen followers?**
☐ Yes.
☐ No

Comments:

3. **Who do you follow on Twitter? Please check all that apply.**

☐ The agency we oversee
☐ Congressional committees
☐ Journalists.
☐ Members of Congress.
☐ We don't follow anyone
☐ Stakeholders.
☐ Other: Please specify

4. **Do you retweet references to your OIG?**

☐ Yes
☐ No

Comments:

Section 7: OIGs That Use Facebook

Please fill out this section if your OIG uses Facebook.

1. **Why does your OIG use Facebook? Please select all that apply.**
   - ☐ It provides us the ability to interact with stakeholders and receive feedback.
   - ☐ Facebook has a large number of users.
   - ☐ Facebook is a source of information for the people we wish to reach.
   - ☐ It provides use with information for use in our audits, investigations, inspections and evaluations.
   - ☐ Other: Please specify.

2. **Do you respond to comments?**

   - ☐ Yes
   - ☐ No

   Please summarize your comments policy here.

3. **Do you screen friend requests?**
   - ☐ Yes
   - ☐ No

4. **Does your OIG allow comments to be posted?**
   - ☐ Yes
   - ☐ No

   Please describe your policy

Section 8: Additional Questions

1. **Are there new media tool(s) that you would like to use as part of your job responsibilities? If so, please explain.**

2. **Do you have any other comments, questions or observations regarding your current or potential use of new media?**

   - ☐ Yes
   - ☐ No

   Please elaborate.

The CIGIE New Media Working Group

The CIGIE New Media Working Group consisted of representatives of the following Offices of the Inspectors General:

Department of Commerce
Department of Education
Department of Health and Human Services
Department of Homeland Security
Department of Housing and Urban Development
Department of Veterans Affairs
Environmental Protection Agency
International Trade Commission
National Aeronautics and Space Administration
National Science Foundation
Pension Benefit Guaranty Corporation
Smithsonian Institution
Social Security Administration
Treasury Inspector General for Tax Administration
United States Postal Service